How to Write a Novel

How to Write a Novel in 90 Days

Conrad Jones

How to Write a Novel

Copyright © 2012 Conrad Jones

All rights reserved.

ISBN: 1482656787
ISBN-13: 9781482656787

How to Write a Novel

CONRAD JONES

HOW TO WRITE A FULL LENGTH NOVEL IN 90 DAYS...... *a tried and tested system used by a successful thriller writer with 12 novels published since 2008!*

BOOK TITLE

How to write a novel in 90 days
Copyright: Conrad Jones
Published: 1st March 2013

Publisher: Gerricon Books/ Createspace
The right of Conrad Jones to be identified as author of this Work has been asserted by her in accordance with sections 77 and 78 of the Copyright, Designs and Patents Act 1988.
All rights reserved. No part of this publication may be reproduced, stored in retrieval system, copied in any form or by any means, electronic, mechanical, photocopying, recording or otherwise transmitted without written permission from the publisher. You must not circulate this book in any format.

Introduction

There are many guides about writing novels on the market but how many of them are written by prolific published authors? The answer is 'not many'. How can anyone write a guide unless they have been through the writing process many times before? The simple answer to this question is they can't because they cannot feed on their own actual experiences to help another writer to avoid the mistakes and pitfalls. Most guides regurgitate information which they have picked up from creative writing books or sites. How can they give you advice when they have never sat down and focused on creating a novel which will sell, many times over? Writing a novel is the same as any other task we undertake as individuals. We have to learn how to do it in order to do it well. When you first learn to drive, you need lessons. No one walks into the kitchen and creates a gourmet dish on their first attempt. If you want a system to apply to writing a book, then you need to take advice from an 'author' who has taken years to develop the process via experience.

When I started writing, I had no idea how I was going to go about it physically. My system was created during the process of writing 9 thrillers, 4 horrors, 2 biographies and over a dozen book marketing guides. I made mistakes and wasted time and if you want to avoid this, then you need to develop a tried and tested system which you can adapt so that it will evolve and morph into your own writing style. I will go into the exact logistics in the next chapter. There is no filling or flannel in this guide, just an exact template to follow which will enable you to create a novel in 90 days or less, depending on how the book flows for you.

The maths

First of all, you need a target to aim for. This target is flexible to a degree but you will need a guide to work by. Short stories can be a few thousand words up to about 15k. Novellas are usually 30-50k but if you are using this guide to create a full length novel then the word count needs to be in excess of 70k. Most publishers are looking for a book which will be about 250-300 pages. Any less, and it's not value for money for their customers. Anymore and it becomes expensive and unprofitable to print and distribute. So let's take a full length novel of 90,000 words.

When the manuscript is finished we need around 300 words on a page. When I write a book I have a much bigger font than this because it's easier on my eyes and makes rewriting and editing simpler. However when it goes to print we are looking for about 250-300 words per page. Don't get too wrapped up in the page count when you are writing because it's almost irrelevant. The word count is what matters to agents and publishers. Stick to measuring your progress using the word count. This point is pivotal to the system of writing a book.

Using 300 words a page we need the book to become 300 pages long, which will give us a novel 90k in length. If we are aiming for completion in 90 days, then we need to set our daily target. Your target is to write 1.5k 'new' words a day. This is flexible too as if you can write more words then great but it is the minimum you need to write. Therefore, in theory you can write a novel in 60 days. This gives you 30 days to take time away from the project and carry on your daily tasks in the real world, which is crucial to your mental state and that of the real people who have to suffer while you create imaginary ones!

When I begin writing a new book, I climb into my 'bubble' and have been known to write for 12 hours a day, 7 days a week for 3 months until it's finished. That is fine for me, as it is my sole occupation but it is difficult for those around me to cope with. If you write in isolation then you must balance writing with the real world.

BOOK TITLE

To recap;

90,000 words

300 words a page

300 pages

1500 new words a day (5 days)

Equates to; 60-90 days for realistic completion target.

Please don't run off to your computer and start writing the first 1.5k words just yet or you will miss the most important part of the writing process!

The hard facts

If you write 1500 words a day and don't rewrite your work, then your book will be gobbledegook. Every novel needs to be rewritten many times over. I will explain how when I go into the system. You must also remember that every novel needs time to develop and grow and you will need time to research your facts and weave them into the fiction. This all takes time if you are going to do it right but if you follow the guidelines then you will have time to spare.

You need to get your story out of your head and onto paper but you will discover that your imagination works much quicker than your hands can write. The best way to do it is to put down your story as it flows from your mind and then when you rewrite, the characters will gain more depth and the story will become richer and deeper as it develops into a novel. Rewriting is a difficult discipline to master because every writer wants to create new pages as quickly as possible. You have to grasp the concept that when you rewrite, you are not just fixing mistakes and editing, you are adding value to your story and creating new words to add to the word count. If you use a system then the discipline will come easily. Writing a book is like any other job you undertake. You have to have procedures and discipline if you are going to take a professional structured approach to creating a novel.

Having a system will teach you how to balance your work with your life outside of your writing bubble. Writing a novel is a long and lonely task and to get from one end to the other successfully, you must have balance and discipline. My first three novels were written in conjunction with running a business. I had to pay the bills at the same time as trying to become a professional author. Making a living from writing is a goal which few authors achieve, so be realistic when you begin your writing plan. Thousands of great books never get published. You need patience and a great deal of luck to make money from one book. Making money from a series of books is dependent on the quality of your first book and how it is received by your readers. If your book is good then you will sell some but there is no guarantee. I will give you a 100% tried and tested method to write your book but after that, your sales will be dependent on how good it is.

The system

1. You have to start with a great idea. What is your book going to be about? People often ask me where my ideas come from. I have written many thrillers and I'm very lucky that my readers still find them exciting. Where do my ideas come from? The truth is that I use things which have 'moved' me in my own life. Things which made me truly 'feel' something inside. Most of the storylines in my novels are from my own personal experiences or from the news. You don't have to look far to find stories which have touched a nation or people across the globe.

Examples from my books;

Soft Target

Was inspired by my personal experiences of witnessing the IRA bombing of Warrington, England in March 1993.

Soft Target 11

Was inspired by the news coverage of the brutal conflict in Chechnya.

Soft Target 111

Was inspired by the news of radioactive material being stolen from the collapsing Soviet Union and its possible use for 'dirty bombs' by extremists.

The Child Taker

Was inspired by the abduction of Madeleine McCann from Portugal whilst on holiday with her parents.

You can get the idea from this selection. Before you start, can you see your story being interesting enough to hold a reader's attention for 300 pages?

2. Start with a bubble page to get the outline on paper. I use a notebook, write the title in the middle of the page and circle it with a bubble. From that central bubble, I write the names of the main characters around it. From each character I join another bubble with their history, parts in the plot and individual characteristics. This bubble page is useful to refer to when you add another character or you mention something specific about an individual or a certain event. Don't worry too much about all the details at this point because the book will change and evolve as you write and rewrite. The initial bubble page is usually nothing remotely like your finished plotline but it is a useful reference in the early stages of creating your characters.
3. On day one, you need to write the first 1.5k words or five pages. Make sure that you make the first pages engaging and exciting. Many readers make up their mind about a novel in the first few pages so make it count.
4. On day two, you need to rewrite the previous day's words and add 1.5k 'new' words to them. You may rewrite your previous pages and find that you have already added 500 new words to the manuscript before starting a new page. This is the beauty of rewriting and usually means that some days you can produce far more words than your target which is a bonus but remember that you will have days where you will struggle to create 1.5k quality words!
5. On day three, you need to rewrite the previous 1.5k words and add 1.5k 'new' words. As you rewrite, your new target of 1.5k words will become shorter as you enhance your earlier chapters thus leaving you less 'new' words to write. Keep to the minimum target and you won't go far wrong. You will find that expanding on your previous day's work will add depth and colour to your novel and eradicate some mistakes too. Make sure you use all five senses when describing scenes and characters. Touch, taste, sight, sound and smells must be conveyed to your readers. Rewriting gives you

the opportunity to turn cardboard characters into living breathing entities, who engage your readers and using descriptive words you can evoke a vivid picture of the settings in the readers' minds.

6. Continue with this process until you reach 10k words and then go back to the beginning and rewrite the book again adding 1.5k new words every day until you reach the end of your 10k words, which will now be significantly more than that. This is the hardest part of the process but it is also the most vital point. Going back to the beginning and adding content will make your book much better. I cannot stress the importance of rewriting enough.

7. Keep on with your target, rewriting the previous day's work until you reach the next milestone of 30k words and then as painful as it might feel, go back to the beginning and repeat the process in point 6. You will find this exercise will significantly develop your novel and the characters will become more lifelike and believable as you paint them and build up their intricate personalities. It also irons out any inconsistencies in the plot as you will become completely entwined in the plot. The more you rewrite the better your book will be and the more the story evolves.

8. Carry on using the same guidelines until you reach the next milestones. At this stage, you can set your own. I use 10k, 30k, 50k, 65k and 80k as the points where I go back to the beginning and rewrite. This method makes your book grow without having to add any fluffing or padding into the storyline. I cannot stress the importance of rewriting. It is the key to writing a good book.

9. Using your work and home commitments to dictate when you can write is important. Try and write at least five days a week but discipline yourself to take two days away from your laptop in every seven days.

10. Remember that if you create 1.5k words every day, you will reach 90k in 60 days. Be realistic in your goal by taking time out every week to develop fresh ideas and clear your head. 90 days is a tough but realistic target to aim for.

Planning and Structure Tips

Goals/Deadlines
5/1/13: Have 5 pages of brainstorming finished
5/15/13: Have an outline finished
5/17/13: Present outline to publisher
6/1/13: 50 pages rough draft
6/30/13: 100 pages rough draft
7/30/13: 150 pages rough draft
8/30/13: 200 pages rough draft
9/1/13: Present rough draft to publisher

Characters
Major: Anna Avery, Louis Avery, Irving Little
Secondary: Laura Avery, Mary Norris, Erica White
Minor Recurring: Rachel Hawthorne, George Hunter, Alan Byrne, Emma Sandstrom, D.J. Williams, Professor Dean

Maps/Settings
General setting: Sarasota, Florida.

Anna and Louis Avery: Single family home in Sarasota, Florida. Ranch style, living and dining room in front, kitchen in middle, two bedrooms in back. Back screened-in porch leads out to sprawling backyard, overgrown with weeds and dead things. Dead end street, neighbor only on one side, older married couple.

Irving Little: Maintenance quarters behind the Mennonite church, 6 blocks from the Avery residence. Small studio apartment on top of a garage full of groundskeeping equipment. Well-kept grounds, lots of flowers and trees, an Eden.

Laura Avery: Retirement home 5 miles from Anna and Louis's home, on the second floor, one small room to herself.

Scenes
Morning Sun Cafe
Avery household
Mennonite Church
Retirement home
Forested area behind Avery household

Research
Ecosystem/weather patterns of Sarasota area
Mennonite church architecture
Mennonite lifestyle
Retirement home statistics, layout, logistics

1. **Pick your moment.** This is not your life story. Your narrative should be something that happened to you that changed you or was significant in some way. The event doesn't have to be huge -- au contraire; sometimes the smaller, simpler events make for more moving outcomes -- but the consequences or your thought process behind it should be. It could be a childhood event, achieving a goal, a failure, or a good or bad deed.[1] If it'd be easy and interesting to write, odds are it'd be a good read.

- Make sure you have a point. Just like writing a paper, your narrative should have a "thesis." After all, if you don't have a point, why should your audience listen to you?[2] There should be a lesson learned or some significant outcome that leaves an impression with your readers.

- Make an outline of the basic parts of your narrative. Because the experience is (most likely) from your memory, there are hundreds of little pieces of information you have to sift through to organize and possibly throw out. Creating an outline will give you the bare bones of your story and help jog your memory in a chronological fashion.

- This is a very, very fine line and even the best of writers may struggle with it. You want to avoid both spelling everything out for the reader (every exhalation of breath, every slight change in color) but you also want to provide vivid details (events need texture, after all). Try to zero in on what's meaningful and what caught your attention. Don't go about fabricating details to achieve poetic eloquence -- you've probably forgotten those things for a reason.

Be aware of your pacing. This doesn't mean setting your treadmill at a certain speed and never deviating from it -- this means knowing when to speed up and slow down. Again, another fine art. But, if the experience is yours, you should have a good idea of when to gloss over the details and when to zero in on what's happening.

- Think of episodes as pearls on a string. Make the pearls full orbed; keep the string stringy. The reader dwells in the episodes, but she needs to be oriented to them, and that is the function of the transitions.[3]

Think about your narrator. This is where the narrative gets interesting. Remember that the narrator isn't necessarily the writer (though it can be) and you can be in the story without narrating it. This gives your narrator the ability to sidestep certain factors (pivotal or otherwise) and be misinformed or flat out wrong. Or even evil.

- When the narrator tells the story in first person, but details in the story lead the reader to suspect that the narrator is not reliable, the result is irony. Irony is a narrative condition in which the reader and the writer share a common judgmental attitude toward the narrator, or when the reader knows more than the narrator and characters in the story.[3]

EditMethod 2 of 3: Writing Your Own Narrative

1. 1

   Get started. Get started right out of the gate. Writing isn't a horse race -- you can't really come up from behind. Get right into the action. Especially at the beginning, avoid long and lengthy descriptions.[4] Your reader needs to be pulled into what's going on -- they won't be appeased by your vocabulary or verbosity.

   - One technique you may want to consider is introducing the experience at the very beginning but holding out on explaining the significance until the end. Your reader's will hopefully be hanging on your every word, waiting for resolution.[1]

2. 2

   Stay organized. It's easy in a narrative to get wrapped up in your thoughts and flashback to related circumstances or jump to the end and leave questions unanswered -- after all, you were there; it's hard to know what you know that others don't. Your outline will help you do this.

   - You are the master of your own narrative, therefore you have all the control and can guide it where you desire. Make sure you're conscious of the fact that you have your entire audience following you, though; don't lead them astray. Have a clear introduction and conclusion.

3. 3

Use your senses. All of them. This is where detail gets vivid and *good*. If you're having trouble describing a person, turn of events, or object, think of your five senses. What do you recall that struck you?

- You may want to start a chart on a piece of scratch paper to get your mind rolling. Have a column each for smells, sounds, sights, tastes, and touch. And just because it's something that's normally attributed to one sense (or two), doesn't mean you can't expand. For example, you can see and hear and feel rain, but the sentence "Virginia rain smells different from a California drizzle."[4] is even more evocative. How would sunscreen taste? How do you see your morning cup of coffee? What did the weather that day *feel* like?

4. 4

Employ consistent and clear language. Much like the descriptive essay, narrative essays are effective when the language is carefully, particularly, and artfully chosen. Use specific language to evoke specific emotions and senses in the reader. Also, keep your audience in mind. A goup of sixth graders will appreciate and perceive different things than a group of business professionals.

- If your narrator isn't you, be especially careful not to slip into your mannerisms. You may not even know what they are! If you are using a third person that has a definite personality or point of view, make a list of their attributes and how they would "talk." Are they biting? Informal? Crude? Pedantic? Once you know these characteristics, you can monitor your writing for them.

EditMethod 3 of 3: Cleaning It Up

1. 1

Take a break. After your work is done, of course. Taking a break is pivotal to refreshing your mind and renewing your eyes. In all the time you've spent writing, your brain has become oblivious to the errors and flow (or lack thereof) in and of your work. Get up, walk around, watch some TV, and come back. You'll notice things you didn't before.

- When you come back, look for errors, yes, but also look for ways that you could be clearer and whether or not your writing helps the readers picture your scene accurately and effectively.[1]

2. 2

Have someone else read your work. Two minds are always better than one. Have a friend or family member who *wasn't* there read your work -- you need an unbiased opinion that has no prior knowledge. This way, they're only using your work as a guide.

- If they're handy with the written word, have them check for spelling, punctuation, and grammatical errors. But also ask them if any questions have been left unanswered, if they can follow along easily, and if they understand the significance of your narrative.

3. 3

Revise and rework. There will probably be some parts that need more detail and parts that need less. Discuss this with your friend -- they're the closest thing you'll get to your real audience.

- Identify and consider removing any information that seems to distract from the focus and main narrative of the essay. It may make sense to you but only confuse the reader. In addition, think about whether you've presented the information in the most effective order. Would it work backwards? Would it work in pieces?
- You may want to title your work. Do this after your narrative has been completely formed -- a title at the beginning may not be the most apt at the end. Check once more for spelling and punctuation errors and submit your work!

Writing Tips

Write Hooks into Your Book

When writing your book, if you want your book to sell you need to look at it from the perspective of the people who you want to read your book. Hundreds of books are published every day and it is difficult to make your book stand out from the rest. Writing hooks in to your book gives readers a reason to pick yours up first. You have to give your target market an incentive to read your work. Think about why they would want to buy it besides the fact that you think it's a good book. What will make them identify with the characters or recognise the sites mentioned in the book? With this in mind (and with your marketing approach in general), start by focusing on your local readers first, whether that is your family and friends or a potential fan base from a large group or organisation connected to you. If you can build a loyal readership in a place of employment, big city or even a small town to start, then you are on a winner.

A good example of this is vicar-turned-author G.P. Taylor and his book *Shadowmancer*. When he completed the manuscript, Reverend Taylor was told no publisher would be interested in a parable about Christianity and black magic set in the eighteenth century. He decided to ignore templated rejection letters from publishers and the naysayers and publish the book himself. He sold his Harley-Davidson to cover the cost of self-publishing the book. The novel's popularity spread gradually by word-of-mouth as parishioners, friends and neighbours recommended it to fellow readers. This local groundswell of support and subsequent positive reviews and media coverage eventually lead Faber & Faber to offering to publish the book, after which it spent fifteen weeks at the top of the British book charts, making Revd Taylor a millionaire and much sought-after literary talent. He sold the US rights to his book for £314,000, which is said to be more than three times J.K. Rowling's US advance for the first Harry Potter story. He then signed a four-year deal for £3.5 million with Faber in the UK and Putnam in the US. The film rights to *Shadowmancer* were sold for £2.25 million, and his book has now been translated into more than twenty different languages.

The lesson of this story is start local, then go regional, national and finally international. You may not have eighty parishioners and God on your side to strengthen your resolve in the marketing of your manuscript, but you will find that your nearest and dearest are often glad to help endorse, review and recommend your book, especially if you add mention of local flavour in a subtle or seemingly disguised way. Remember that word-of-mouth will sell more books than any other media. If a fan of your novels tells their family and friends that a local landmark or street name, river, cathedral or train station is in the story, then they can visualise the book as it progresses. It also gives you a hook into the local media, which is really important.

Local landmarks, street names or areas will give you a hook into the local media vehicles. You will have to try to build personal relationships with local journalists, editors, radio personalities and their associates, which are priceless when you are releasing a new book or have a book-signing coming up. So if you have a local interest in your book, then the press are more willing to listen to you when you call. An important point to remember is unless you're a celebrity, your book is not news however interesting and informative it is until you've built up a grassroots following. Don't be disappointed if your local television station does not call you back or your local newspaper leaves you on hold until you finally hang up. Any successful author has had more doors slammed in their face than they can remember but as your local fan base and social network grows, then so does the news value. When any author launches their first book, nobody wants to know; you have to start on the bottom rung and take one step up the ladder at a time, working hard at building interest in you as a brand. Writing hooks into your books helps to achieve this.

If you have links any to large organisations, then mention them in the book. For example, at the end of Conrad Jones's *Soft Target*, the local football derby is targeted by terrorists. Liverpool is a city full of football fans, blue and red. We are talking about millions of fans. Using the clubs in the book gave it a hook into the corporate side of the clubs and they invited Conrad to do book signings at their pre-match corporate dinners. Likewise, incorporating a scuba diving centre in the Lake District, which has thousands of members, also helped to generate sales of the book in the early days. They distributed bookmarks and sent email to their members telling them that the dive centre was mentioned in his book. These hooks are case specific but the key point is to think about the content of your book and look for the hooks that can get your foot in the door. Conrad didn't put these places and organisations into the story by accident; he did it intentionally to make marketing his book easier. Use the places in your book to help you reach pockets of interest.

Similarly, you should place the names of friends, family and your main readers in your ebook. You can use given names or second names only if they have asked you to put them into the storyline. If you want someone to tell everyone that they meet about your book, put them in it. It's often said that when someone looks at a photo, the first person they look for is themself. Similarly, if you subtly mention one of your friends or fans in your book (not just in the acknowledgements, but in the narrative itself), you'll be surprised at how favourable they'll review your book and how many times they'll mention it to others, and there's nothing better than a good recommendation, which is known today as "viral marketing".

Be careful not to associate their character with their names but if done correctly, this generates word of mouth and builds sales. For instance, if your brother is named Stanley Timothy Parker and you write thrillers, you might want to add in Major Stanley Timms to the terrorist taskforce. Another example is Sylvia Blythe, a detective in *The Child Taker*. The name is the maiden name of a big fan who also writes reviews for every novel that Conrad writes. If you can build that kind of loyalty from readers then you will sell ebooks to the people they talk to and good recommendations and reviews are priceless. Hooks help sell books.

Hit the Ground Running

You need to grab the attention of your reader in the first paragraph so they'll want to read more. If you spend too much time in setting the scene and developing the characters, you'll lose your readers after a few pages. Rather, you need to grab their attention and hold it throughout your book. Let your characters through their dialogue and actions convey to the reader about what's around them, what situation they're in and who they are. If you look at your story objectively and don't believe that the first chapter excites or intrigues the reader (with novels) or informs the reader (with non-fiction), change it or create a prologue that does.

Your opening sentence, opening paragraph, opening page will set the tone for the rest of your book. If your book starts at a gradual pace and builds up momentum and leads to an unforgettable twist at the end, the problem is that some readers and reviewers will read the beginning and not bother to read on. Start with an action scene in novels rather than setting the scene and introducing the characters; start straight in with practical tips or advice with business books/guides rather than spending the first few chapters explaining the theory behind the practice. Hook your readers on the first page and make sure that you add hooks on every few pages and keep the action moving so that they stay captivated throughout the book.

Exercise 1. Take half an hour to think about the names and places in your book. Could you place marketing hooks into it?

For example:

Could a female character in the book have their name tweaked to become your sister, auntie, friend, work colleague?

Could a character visit a local landmark or could you mention a famous street name in the novel?

Are there any football teams, organisations, companies or recognisable brands mentioned in the text?

Choose Your Words Carefully

You can write a masterpiece that is worthy of literary accolades and awards the world over but if it does not speak to your target audience then you are wasting your time creating it in the first place. Be careful to keep your story flowing and the language understandable. If readers have to look up more than one word in a chapter then the writer has already lost their interest. Using longwinded flowery sentences can irritate readers as can the use of obscure words, which have to be explained.

A classic example of this is Stephen Hawkings's *A Brief History of Time*. Hawking approached an editor with his ideas for a popular book on cosmology. The editor was doubtful about all the equations in the draft manuscript, which he felt would put off laypersons and buyers in airport bookshops that Hawking hoped to reach. The editor warned him that for every equation in the book the readership would be halved, eventually persuading Hawking to drop all but one equation: $E = mc^2$. In addition to Hawking's notable abstention from presenting equations, the book also simplifies matters by means of illustrations throughout the text, depicting complex models as diagrams. No doubt Stephen was frustrated by the editor's demands but the commercial aspect of the book has to be the priority.

You can find similar problems in Robert Ludlum's Bourne thrillers. The films are full of non-stop action and are ultra-exciting but the books are difficult to read and the vocabulary is over-complicated. Keep it simple; the storyline is more important to the reader than your superior knowledge of vocabulary or insider jargon.

Don't get too wordy. With ebooks you can provide a good amount of information in a succinct way. Resist the urge to weave in too many plots or offer too much conventional wisdom unless it is specifically pertinent to the main storyline or product or service that you are selling and then, only if it is relevant/applicable to the target audience. Descriptions of characters and places are important but keep the narrative flowing as you can lose the reader by being overly descriptive and too clever with overly complicated plotlines or delivering an overdose of unexpected twists.

Authors often write novels with characters speaking in their local dialect, which can make it difficult to read (especially if you don't speak the local dialect) and slow the pace of the book. It's like having subtitles in movies – people generally go to see action movies to relax and be entertained, not to have to read off the screen and therefore miss some of the action. Likewise, if a reader is struggling to follow the discourse or dialogue in a novel, they're much more likely to put down the book than take the time to learn the lingo. A great example of how to include authentic character-spoken accents without causing readers to struggle to understand the local dialect is *Moby Dick* by Herman Melville.

Similarly, it's generally a good idea to temper too much crude language in action novels, which might put off or offend potential readers. In *The Bourne Identity*, there are thirty uses of the word "s—t", two uses of the word "f—k", a few uses of "damn", "hell", and over a dozen exclamatory uses of God's name in vain. Do they really add to the atmosphere or action? In hard-hitting or gritty books like *Trainspotting* or *Porno* by Irvine Welsh there needs to be the right measure of expletives to accurately reflect the language used by the characters, but if the book is replete with harsh language or expletives on most every page, it'll put off readers, retailers and magazine reviewers (with ebooks, e-tailers and e-zines reviewers).

Exercise 2. Are there words in your book that can limit your readership? Will a layperson reading your book have to either pass over the words without knowing what they mean (and thus the meaning is lost) or take the time to look up the words in the dictionary (and thus the flow is lost)?

Can you change them to everyday speak to broaden your readership? If the language is only understandable to some, can you change it so it is understandable to many? Are you using terminology to try to distinguish yourself or terms that might be offensive to your readers? If so, your book will have limited appeal.

Show Not Tell

Allow your readers to experience the story through actions, thoughts, senses and feelings rather than through author exposition, summarisation and description. Don't drown the reader in adjectives, but allow readers to experience your ideas by interpreting events in the story. Nobel Prize-winning novelist Ernest Hemingway was a notable proponent of the "show, don't tell" style. In his own words, "The dignity of movement of an iceberg is due to only one-eighth of it being above water." The "dignity" Hemingway speaks of suggests a form of respect for the reader, who should be trusted to develop a feeling for the meaning behind the action without having the point painfully laid out for them.

As alluded to previously, rather than setting each scene and portraying the landscape through detailed descriptions, let your characters set the atmosphere and scene through their own words, and define themselves through their actions. Let your characters tell the story, rather than you telling it for them from a third-party perspective. If you use the narrative to paint the scene, your book will read like a film script. Your readers need to get into the minds of the characters and identify with them, but if you're describing it then they'll feel removed from the action.

Think about writing in an active voice rather than using passive descriptions. Adding just a few key phrases here and there could make all the difference to your novel.

For instance:

Asda was busy that day, packed with shoppers. (Passive)

'I could barely move in Asda that day; the other shoppers streamed up and down the aisles like rats in a maze,' Stephanie said in an irritated tone. (Active)

Both sentences say the same thing but the second is spoken by a character in the book; this both gives her and the narrative more depth and allows the reader to visualise her speaking. Remember that readers like "show, don't tell" so be careful not to overuse the narrative to describe the setting when you could use a key character to do it better, while giving depth to the character at the same time.

For instance:

The woods looked dark and spooky as the light faded. (Tell)

Sarah turned and looked towards the woods. The dark shadows made her shiver with fear as the sun sank behind the mountain. (Show)

Once again, both sentences say the same thing but the second allows us to visualise the scene and get a sense of what the character was feeling at the time. On a similar theme, when establishing the year in which the chapter is set, you can use a brief description in the narrative or, preferably, you could use the action to show the reader what year it is.

For instance:

Paul left school in 1983 and could still vividly remember the journey home after his last day. (Tell)

Paul remembered the day he left school like it was yesterday. He had said goodbye to his best friend when his uncle turned up at the bus stop in his brand new 1983 plate Ford Capri. 'Nice car, Uncle Dave, have you been robbing banks again?' Paul had teased.

'Just picked it up this morning. Get in and less of your cheek or you can walk home,' his uncle grumbled. (Show)

Exercise 3. Consider the following: Place, time and setting

There are two essential dimensions to the setting of any book: place and time. If you have written a novel set in the present, the time in which your story is set is relatively straightforward and the tenses used are easy to check. However, if you are writing fiction that spans the lifetime of a character or goes back to events of a character's past then you will need to pay special attention to tenses to ensure readers always know what time each chapter or paragraph is set in or it could easily become confusing.

Do not take it for granted that the reader knows where the story is up to and avoid having more than one person speaking in any single paragraph as it can leave readers wondering who is speaking at any given point in the narrative. You will know who is speaking as the author, but the reader may not.

Add Depth and Colour to Your Characters

Every character in your book will have many dimensions but have you described them fully, irrespective of their role in the plot? You know the characters, what they look like, what they wear and what their traits are, but have you conveyed this to readers? Are they relaxed and laid back or dark and dangerous? Could a few more adjectives give them more depth and make your book a better read?

Another dimension often left under described are the places and things that have a presence, despite not being "living" things.

For instance:

New York, vibrant, exciting, noisy but dark and dangerous at times.

London, historic, multicultural, old, tired and scruffy around the seams.

The harvest moon, glowing, mysterious, with a dark side.

Honda Fire Blade, powerful, unforgiving, eye-catching lines.

Use descriptive "humanising" words for some inanimate objects as well as your human characters. Some writers do not pay due attention to the setting because they are keen to get stuck into the storyline. You know where the story takes place and the setting is a clear in your mind, but is that clarity of vision conveyed through the writing? You can be sure that a drab setting is dull and one-dimensional at best and unclear or confusing at worst. You have to make sure the reader knows where he or she is at every juncture, and your descriptions should help them navigate their way through the scenes alongside your characters. You can be subtle or you can be direct as long as you use good descriptions along the way.

For example:

John crossed the street, wearing a black suit and carrying a holdall. Beneath his arm was a copy of the local newspaper.

The setting, time and place could be enhanced considerably with the use of some "show" techniques and some well-placed adjectives.

John had to wait for a line of black-cabs to roar by before he could cross the street. As he reached the halfway point, a double-decker splashed rainwater over his highly polished shoes and the trousers of his black suit were soaked to the knees. The Adidas holdall, which he was carrying, felt heavy. Beneath his arm was a copy of the local paper, the Manchester Evening News.

Exercise 4. Spend a half hour taking one paragraph from each chapter in your book and enhance the setting or add depth to the characters.

Make use of your characters' five senses to enhance the setting. This applies throughout the manuscript but especially when your characters are in places like the dark, woods, undercover, and so on. Describing the sights, sounds and smells will enrich the scene for your readers. If the characters are on the beach or in a fish-and-chip shop, a fun fair or a morgue, what stench or aroma can they smell? Smells are evocative when setting the scene, so do not underestimate how powerful writing them into the setting can be.

Pick a paragraph in your book and imagine what sounds you would hear while the action was taking place. You do not have to be over descriptive but the odd line here and there will add more depth to your narrative. If you characters are in the woods, can they hear the breeze in the trees? If they are near the sea, are the waves lashing against the rocks? If they are on a bridge near a railway station, could they feel the rush of air from a passing train? During a fight scene, can they feel the crowd closing in on them?

Novels *should* have colourful characters with vibrant scenes, and rich characters and colourful scenes, that are smelly, fragrant, noisy, silent, silky, slimy, bitter, sweet – and always highly visual. Write from your characters' perspectives and don't assume the reader knows what's in your mind, that he or she can imagine what the characters are feeling. Show the readers your imaginative world through the characters' eyes.

Exercise 5. Check if your characters are using their senses fully in your book. What can they see, feel, smell and taste?

Check Your Facts

Research is vital and a lack of proper research is a mistake made by many authors. Readers are intelligent and if you insult their intelligence with a blatant anachronism then it will spoil their enjoyment of your book. If your character is holding a Glock 17, then make sure you know it fires 9 mm ammunition and how many bullets can be slotted into a magazine. That may sound obvious to some but if you mention that your character "flicked off the safety catch and opened fire" then some clever-clogs will inevitably review your book and point out that a Glock 17 doesn't have a safety. If you are not sure, Google it. All the information any writer could ever need is available on the Internet. If you are writing about a meeting at the White House, chances are that you have never been in there and neither have your readers. However, a quick look on Google images will show you the colour of the wallpaper and which pictures are actually on the walls. To add authenticity, you can add a single well-researched detail.

For instance:

John gazed up from the desk at Lincoln's portrait and his fingers felt the scorch mark left on the veneer by Clinton's cigar.

Both facts are made up but your readers need to believe that you know what you are writing about to be convinced by the storyline. Suggesting that President Clinton burnt the veneer is difficult to verify and hints that you have an intimate knowledge of the Oval Office. So don't be afraid to take some liberties. Invent just what you need to set the scene but keep it real. Make sure you give clear facts, and keep them pithy and precise. If you use real events in your book to make it seem authentic, then make sure you know the details.

Also, be careful with the overuse of clichés. The English language is full of clichés and we are all guilty of using them unwittingly. Clichés are nothing other than laziness and readers don't usually respond well if a book is riddled with them. Instead of saying "The worst case scenario", just say "at worst". Rather than saying "At the end of the day", better to say "ultimately". And don't overuse the thesaurus. There's a temptation to always search for a synonym. But generally, the simple more direct word is better. Show that you know, but don't show off what you know.

Exercise 6. Revisit some of the "factoids" or descriptions stated in your book and research them further. When in doubt, always look it up and add more facts to the story, not to impress readers but to convince them you know what you're writing about.

~~~~~~~~~~~~~~~~~~~~~~~

Now that you have:

- written hooks into your book
- hit the ground running
- chosen your words wisely
- shown rather than told
- added depth, colour and sense
- turned factoids into facts

Your book can now be proofread, formatted and uploaded as an ebook.

Have Your Manuscript Proofed

If you have written a short story, novella, full-length non-fiction book or novel, then your document's word count will run into the thousands. You will have spent months staring at the written pages, creating, developing, expanding and then editing your precious work. The problem is that as writers, at the final stage when we want to make sure that our book is the very best it can be, we are often too close to it so we tend to read *what we think that we have written, not exactly what we have written* and this applies to both the storyline and the grammar. No matter how many times you have read through your book, there will be room for improvement.

Before you convert your document into an ebook, you need readers to content edit the storyline, and not just for punctuation, spelling and grammar. There are few things more frustrating for authors than spending hours and hours writing and proofreading their own work, only for reviewers to point out poor phrasing or wording, anachronisms, inconsistencies and overlooked grammatical and spelling mistakes. You want readers to positively review your book based on its literary merits, not adversely review it based on deficient formatting or grammar. Regardless of how many times you have read over it yourself, fresh eyes will find mistakes in it.

How many times have you seen poor reviews because of the production of the book? Add to that the number of negative reviews because of "wooden dialogue" or "cardboard characters" even if the reviewer thinks that the premise of the book was good? Pick any fictional novel from the top 100 sellers and click on the reviews. Check the one-star reviews and you will see that there are consistent themes that reviewers pick up on and they are listed in the pages below. To help avoid this happening to your ebook and give it the very best chance of commercial success, before you convert your book into ebook format or e-publish your book, you need to have it content edited in the following ways:

1. Make sure that you have spellchecked the document in its entirety without ever clicking on the "ignore rule" tab, otherwise the programme will skip over some basic mistakes. Sometimes the grammar checks miss obvious mistakes on the first check, so having it repeated by someone else is always worthwhile.
2. Make sure at least one other person other than a friend or family member has spellchecked the document as above, and read the story as a reader would. Friends and family may tell you what you want hear and that may not always be a true reflection of the quality of your work. Protecting your feelings may be their primary concern rather than giving you an honest critique.
3. There are many simple mistakes that the spellcheck does not always find. Checking them using the Find function can save you some heartache later on. Using the Find function, check the use of the following words.

Exercise 7. Take a half hour to spellcheck your manuscript and check out the following commonly misspelled words and their context:

    there, their, they're

were, where, we're
your, you're
its, it's
quit, quite, quiet
to, too
whose, who's
rain, reign, rein
fair, fare
fro, for, from
desert, dessert
affect, effect
than, then
chose, choose
whose, who's
lose, loose

Make sure your spellcheck is using United Kingdom English and not United States. Although differences are subtle, if you are inconsistent through the work, then it will annoy your readers.

Stumbling blocks

You will obviously have days where you will struggle to create anything of substance. I have been lucky because writer's block hasn't bothered me at any point so far in my writing career. I genuinely believe that this is because I rewrite so often. Going back through the manuscript creates new ideas and develops old ones. Rewriting is the true cure for any mental block.

As I explained earlier, writing is my occupation but it wasn't always so. Day to day issues can get in the way of your writing if you are not careful. We all know how it is. You've spent ages thinking about what you're going to do that day and you have scheduled a few hours to write, anticipating it, feeling frustrated because other things are getting in the way of it. Finally, you switch on your computer or get out your pen and paper to expand your bubble pages when the phone rings or there is a knock at the door. Worse still, you have something urgent on your mind. Money issues or health problems are things we all have to navigate and having something burning in your mind could lead to a day where the words won't come, or they seem laughably trite or clichéd or flaccid. When you are struggling to write new content and you cannot focus then it is easy to become overcome by the urgent need to sort out the washing or phone the gas supplier, who is threatening to cut off the supply. If you use a laptop then it is too easy to logon and surf a favourite website looking for inspiration. Maybe you could call that research but if you are wandering aimlessly then it is better to go back to beginning and rewrite. Remember that you have a few days a week to play with and if it isn't coming then turn off your computer and walk away. Have a coffee or put the burning issues to bed with a few phone calls and then sit down focuses and refreshed and rewrite. Rewrite, rewrite and rewrite!

The first chapters you write are just the bones of the skeleton of your novel. Remember that you are going to go over your work multiple times so it doesn't have to be perfect at first. Punctuation, grammar and syntax are all usually very good in traditionally published books because they have been through the industry process, edited and copy edited by experts. I am a storyteller and no more than that. I expect my traditionally published books to be as near perfect as they can be however my self-published books have not had that kind of polishing. If you want every sentence to be perfect as soon as you've written it, or you fret that your grasp of apostrophes isn't all it could be, you will probably agonise over every word so much that the flow will soon dry up. Right now, you need to get the words down. The editing stage can come later.

Getting your story out of your head is the most important way to get started. Rewriting will give you the opportunity to build on the characters. Creating characters isn't easy and it is in fact one of the hardest and most essential jobs in writing. The main way to write really strong characters is to know them inside out - at least as well as yourself because every character in your book has been created by you. Rewriting will allow you to get to know them inside out. Make sure that you use your bubble pages to develop your characters and keep them updated daily as you add to them. Write down everything you know about your central characters and you will find new ideas and inspiration will come naturally.

If you find yourself struggling then develop your descriptions of the scenes and settings so that the readers can envisage every detail. I use real landmarks and places in my stories, which endears readers from those areas to you. Researching a place or town in your book takes only minutes but it will give you a sentence or two which will enrich your writing dramatically. Don't go overboard on the history too much. A line or two is plenty.

Think about adding marketing hooks into your storyline

If you have any links to large organisations, then use them in the book. At the end of *Soft Target*, the local football derby is targeted by terrorists. Liverpool is a city full of football fans, blue and red. I am talking about millions of fans. Using the clubs in my book gave me a hook into the corporate side of the clubs and they invited me to do book signings at their pre-match corporate dinners. I also incorporated a scuba diving centre in the Lake District, which has thousands of members. They distributed bookmarks and sent e-mails to their members. These tips are case specific but the key point to it is to think about the content of your book and look for the hooks which can get your foot in the door. Use the places in your book to help you reach pockets of interest.

Most of my books have the names of friends, family and more recently some of my readers in them. I use their Christian names or second names usually because they have asked me to put them into the storyline. If you want someone to tell everyone that they meet about your book, put them in it. Be careful not to associate their character with their names but if done correctly, this generates word of mouth and builds sales. For instance, my brother is called Stanley Timothy Jones. I use a Major in the terrorist taskforce named Stanley Timms. Another example is Sylvia Blythe, a detective in *The Child Taker*. The name is the maiden name of one of my biggest fans who also puts reviews on every novel. If you can build that kind of loyalty from readers then you will sell books to the people they talk to and good reviews are priceless. You will be amazed how many of your friends and family promise to put a review on Amazon and never get around to it.

Hit the ground running. You need to grab the attention of your reader in the first paragraph so they'll want to read more. If you look at your story objectively and don't believe that the first chapter excites or intrigues the reader, change it or create a prologue which does. I have met dozens of readers at book signings who like my books because they start on page one rather than page fifty-one. Hook them on the first page and make sure that they stay hooked throughout the book.

Don't get too wordy. With eBooks you can provide a good amount of information in a succinct way. Resist the urge to tell too many stories unless they are specifically pertinent to the product or service that you are selling and then, only if they are applicable to the target audience. Descriptions of characters and places are important but keep the storyline flowing. Pace and plot are vital.

Summary

90,000 words novel

300 pages

300 words a page

Set up you bubble pages

1500 words a day minimum

Rewrite the previous day's words everyday

Use milestones to go back to the beginning

Keep your bubble pages updated

Rewrite when you are struggling to create new content.

Write 5 days in every 7

Take 2 days a week off

Balance your writing with those around you

Tips on grammar

Use the full point after abbreviations and contractions only where the last letter is not the final letter of the word: No., Capt., a.m., p.m., i.e., e.g. (upper- and lower-case). And for personal initials: W.B.Yeats

The full point is omitted thus: Mr, Dr, St, Ltd; after sets of initials: BBC, NATO, MP and also after abbreviated units of measurement: ft, in, m, km, lb, g

Capitalisation

Aim for the minimum use of capitalisation. Generally, however, the following are capped:

Specific organisations and groups, institutions and religious bodies: the Labour Party, but the party, the Church believes, but the church nearby, Buddhism, Buddhist, Islam, Muslim

Titles and ranks where a specific individual is named: Queen Charlotte, but a queen, all lords, no bishops, kings of England

Historical periods, wars and economic or political periods: Neolithic, Stone Age, the Second World War, the Depression

Geographical locations recognized as social/political regions: the Midlands, the West Country, but the north, the south-west

Figures and Numbers

Write numbers below 100 in words (except where the author is comparing numbers or recording a unit of measurement); 100 and above as numerals: 2 cats and 144 dogs, six dogs and eighty-six cats; I could see for 6 miles

For collective numbers use the least number of figures possible: 1944-5, 1986-93, 1997-2003. But note: 1990-95, 16-17, 116-17

Set dates: 1 February 1950, in the late nineteenth century (but late-nineteenth century war), the eighties, the 1980s, but in the 1970s and '80s. AD (preceding date) and BC (following date)

Set times of the day: four o'clock, 11.15 a.m., 7.45 p.m., a quarter to eight, half past nine

Italics

Use italics for the titles of books, book-length poems, newspapers and magazines; works of performed art, television and radio programmes; names of ships.

Follow the Oxford Guide to Style for foreign and anglicised words and use italics for emphasis sparingly.

Layout

The first line of a chapter should normally be set full out. A new section, following a one-line space, also should be set full out. Text which follows an extract or verse quote, also full out, unless this impairs the sense, in which case it should be indented as a new paragraph.

However, the layout of headings, quotations and lists, the order and content of preliminary matter and the construction of notes and references must be retained.

Punctuation

Aim to 'correct grammar, to impose consistency, and to clarify – not alter – meaning'. All general rules are dealt with in the Oxford Guide to Style. Some points that may cause difficulty are:

Apostrophe

Possessives: The inclusion or omission of the possessive s should be decided on the grounds of euphony; this means that some possessives will have an s and some will not, but there should be some system. The Oxford

Guide recommends that (except in ancient names)'s should be used in all monosyllables and disyllables, and in longer words accented on the penultimate syllable. Also,'s should be used except when the last syllable of the word is pronounced iz: Bridges', Moses', but James's, Thomas's.

Watch out for the incorrect apostrophe in its, yours, ours, theirs, hers

Plurals: Do not use the apostrophe when creating plurals: the Joneses (not the Jones's); the 1990s (not the 1990's); QCs (not QC's). Do not employ what is sometimes known as the 'greengrocer's apostrophe': orange's for oranges and cauli's for cauliflowers

No apostrophe in phone, plane, bus, flu etc.

Dashes and ellipses

For parenthetical dashes, use spaced en rules

For the omission of part of a word, or for abruptly curtailed speech, use a closed-up em rule

For the omission of a whole word, use a spaced em rule

Ellipses should be spaced thus… with a full point at the end of the sentence, if relevant

Hyphenation

Do not hyphenate unnecessarily.

Use hyphens to avoid ambiguity: a little used car or a little-used car; when employing words attributively: an ill-informed person; in phrasal compounds: jack-in-the-box; in compound adjectives preceding a noun: working-class hero; where part of the compound is a measurement: 9-mile run

Omit hyphens when employing words predicatively: that person is ill informed; when the first word of the compound is an adverb: widely known facts; or where the compound is a name: Iron Age fort

Quotations

Preferably use single quotation marks, reserving double quotes for a quote within a quote but the decision is the author's.

Place punctuation marks in relation to quotation marks according to sense. The closing inverted comma precedes all punctuation except an exclamation mark, question mark, dash or ellipsis belonging to the quotation. Where a full sentence, with an initial capital, is quoted at the end of a main (author's) sentence, the full point should precede the inverted comma.

In dialogue the punctuation is always placed inside the punctuation marks: 'It is,' he said, 'a great album.'

Closing parenthesis

A full point should precede a closing parenthesis only if the parentheses enclose a complete sentence which is not part of a longer sentence. A question mark or exclamation mark may precede or follow a closing parenthesis as the sense demands. A comma, colon, semicolon or a parenthetical dash should never precede a closing parenthesis.

Spelling

Use the Shorter Oxford English Dictionary. There is an online dictionary resource from OUP: www.askoxford.com or refer to the Oxford Guide to Style for alternative spellings, unusual words or short foreign phrases. Collective nouns are singular, e.g. company, government. Verbs used with them must also be singular.

Optional endings: -ise or -ize (author's choice)

Retain American spelling for proper names: Pearl Harbor, Rockefeller Center

EXTRA BITS

Online Promotional Tips

eBook Marketing in the Virtual World

When you are preparing your marketing plans, timing is crucial. If you are looking for a magic formula to sell 10,000 copies of your book, then you'll be disappointed. There is no one solution. You have to use the shotgun method, during which you are aiming multiple activities at the same target. Whether you are about to launch or re-launch your book, you have to spend some time planning all your promotional activities and making sure that you co-ordinate them for maximum effect.

Build up interest in your launch weeks before the actual date but make sure that your book is uploaded and available prior to the launch. Don't waste media opportunity by announcing in July that your book will be available from next Christmas because unless you are already a household name, no one will remember.

You need to set up a checklist where you can record your activities, set completed-by dates and tick each activity off when it's accomplished. Never throw the checklist away as you can use it for reference in years to come. Keep as much detail as you can until you have experimented with the format that works for you. For example:

Activity	When	Completed	Comments/results

Send out bookmarks to local readers' group Birchwood readers c/o 44 holly drive wa4 6yu Appleton Book Club c/o 42 willis rd wa5 4qz	1 week before launch	yes	Received invitation to present at their March meeting. Contact Dave Mann 07768957687
Contact Susan at Radio Merseyside 0151-487-0000 susan@bbc.radio	1 week after launch	Called Tuesday	Appearing on Susan's show 5/2/2012
Send letters to colleges in North Wales	2 months before launch	Sent out 23 letters/	Had 15 replies and two invites to present in March

I used a daily, weekly, monthly and six-monthly to-do list to keep me organised. For example:

Daily	Weekly	Monthly	6 Monthly
Check sales reports			
Record any comments on highs and lows	Send out batch of 20 letters	Update contact lists	Update local radio
Check book reviews and reply to the reviewer	Send out bookmarks	Update marketing plan	Update local TV
Check Facebook and update status. Reply to any messages	Update book reviews on goodreads	Update local newspaper	

As a writer, it's all too easy to become totally encapsulated in writing your next book and thereby neglect your marketing plan, which is paramount to the commercial success of your book. And until you are disciplined enough to follow a monthly routine automatically use a 'to-do' list daily.

Do not spend any money on advertising in the press or with companies who pertain to send out press releases for you. I published *Soft Target* as a paperback with one of the biggest international self-publishing companies around. They offered some marketing packages, which on paper looked amazing but in reality I spent £3,000 that I didn't have without seeing any tangible return on my investment.

You will be keen and enthusiastic about getting your message to as many people as possible and paying someone to do it for you appears to be the easy option but I guarantee that you will waste your money, especially if you are an independent author. Most blanket press releases don't make it past the spam filters and as we said before, your book is not news yet.

I paid a small fortune to my publishers and they promised to distribute press releases to newspapers and radio stations all across the USA and UK. That was in 2008 and I'm still waiting for the phone to ring from the media sources confirming receipt of the press release and requesting an interview. Don't waste your money; you will have to do this yourself.

Similarly, I met a self-published thriller writer who had a personal friend working in the advertising department at a glossy men's monthly magazine – let's call it HFM. It is a well-established publication with a huge readership. His friend secured him a double-page spread advertising his book for free. It sounded like an author's dream come true; two glossy pages to advertise your book with an editorial about the author and the plot. I was insanely jealous and could not wait to see the results of such a press campaign. He ordered hundreds of hard copies of his novel in anticipation of the sales rush for his books. All his internet sellers were stocked up and ready to go and his eBook was uploaded and polished to perfection.

When the magazine came out, he logged online every hour on the hour to check sales. Nothing happened, in actual fact he sold less copies that month than in the month before. The advertising space would have cost him £1000s. He was devastated by the result but if he actually bought that advert, I think he would have thrown himself under the number 23 bus.

Social Media and Social Networking

Use the power of social media to spread the word about your eBook. The internet is the key to let an unknown author place their novel next to the biggest names in the literary world. If you use it correctly, you can generate a lot of interest in your books. If you get it wrong, you will become an annoying internet troll harassing everyone. It is a fine line so do be careful. Be polite at all times even when people criticise your work. Remain positive and friendly or you will lose readers when you are trying to gain them and endear people to you as the author.

Social media marketing also termed as SMO has become a popular tool to promote just about everything that you can possibly think of. Sites like Twitter, Facebook, YouTube, MySpace, LinkedIn, Ning, Bebo and various blogs and vBlogs all allow authors to "repost" or share information about themselves and their eBook easily. Since the same information is shared by a reader with their contacts and hopefully by contacts of their contact, it helps in spreading the word fast thus reaching more and more potential readers.

Remember that bad news travels faster than good so be careful when interacting with readers. I have witnessed some long winded exchanges on book review sites which would make you cringe. Eventually the argument becomes the focus rather than the book or the review. Social networking sites act as word-of-mouse (viral) promotion adding more value to your book so do not underestimate the damage you could do by being obtuse. Third-party endorsements are the best recommendation that you can hope for and readers love it when you comment on their review of your book, even if it is a poor review. Remember that they have spent their money buying your book, invested their time reading it and then taken the time to sit down and write a review. They are entitled to their opinion.

A social network facilitates regular communication between individuals who are connected by friendship or common interest. Most common interest manifests itself as a group. All you have to do is search keywords linked to your book and you will find groups to join. You can use these networks to enhance your personal network, and grow sales. The key is to use all appropriate functions of a given social network for maximum benefit.

Facebook (www.facebook.com) allows you to create a profile, join groups of people with similar interests, discuss your personal interests, and communicate with friends and potential customers. Facebook is massive and is a gift to the unknown author. Every author should be on Facebook.

If you already have a Facebook page then hopefully you have established the basics. Go to the "search friend" space at the top of your profile and type in kindle. Over 20 groups will appear and you need to join them all. Some of them will be invitation only but you can request an invite.

Build your profession into your Facebook name. For example mine is "Conrad Jones bestselling kindle author". That is not for vanity; it's because I want people to know that they have found the right Conrad Jones and when I request to join a writing group, it is obvious that I have something to offer the group.

When you have joined a group, make sure that you interact in a positive manner and add the other members as friends. This way your profile as a writer is growing and you are reaching dozens and dozens of people who are interested in books. Do not just join and post a link to your Amazon page and then disappear or you will turn people off you very quickly. Joining a group for shameless self-promotion will not gain you any fans; in fact, it's likely to have the opposite effect.

Using the search bar, type in authors and writers, dozens of groups will appear. Join them and follow the steps above. Add their members to your friends list and remember that the more friends you have and the more interesting your posts are, the more people will be interested in you and your books. Just introduce yourself to the group and express the desire to talk to other authors and readers about writing and promoting books. Mention that you are looking for reviewers to give you feedback. Don't forget to send speedy replies to any communication you receive.

Once again, search but type in readers this time but you must be careful with readers' sites. Readers' sites detest self-promotion, especially from unknown self-published authors. I know from experience they can be easily offended. Join as many groups as possible and add as many friends from those groups as you can and then dedicate time every day to update and inform people about your books and launch dates by updating your profile status.

Increase your friends and contact list and then set up an event, which will be the launch of your eBook. Make sure you set up a Twitter (*www.twitter.com*) account and a LinkedIn (*www.linkedin.com*) site before you set up your event as they all link through the same page on Facebook. Once again, if you aren't familiar with these sites, then take ten minutes to take a look at them and familiarise yourself with how they work. It will probably take you fifteen minutes to half an hour to set yourself up with a profile when you are ready to.

Set up your author page on Amazon by going to the Author Central page, and link it to your Twitter and Facebook pages. All you do is click on the icons and the software does the rest for you. Along with your blog, these three sites are crucial to any internet campaign. Build your profiles with pictures, book covers and reviews. Keep it fun and interesting and people will be regular visitors to your site.

If you are getting ready to publish a book then you have to "get up to speed" with social media marketing. A lot of authors I talk to want to learn about social media and how it's going to help them sell thousands of books but they hesitate, because they're not confident with it. They know they need to be building their author platform and brand, but don't know how Twitter fits in. It's a simple platform to send regular updates and build an audience. There are only a few things you can actually do on Twitter but simple is good. Everything else that flows from your involvement with it comes from the network of people you connect with.

It takes time and effort to build a following. If you have no followers then you are wasting your time. You have to grow a community around the value of the content and ideas you share on the site.

On Twitter, make sure your username name is not random or too long, 10 or 12 characters should do. Remember that your username on Twitter needs to include author or writer in it if you're going to use it for promoting your book. It is part of your branding strategy.

There is free software that makes Twitter a lot easier to use. Twitterific on the iPad and the iPhone are good, though there are many others so it's worth looking around to see what works for you. The software allows you to automate your Twitter profile which saves time.

Being able to schedule Tweets in advance is a big advantage and you can auto-tweet which gives you the ability to plan a campaign.

Here are some pointers for using Twitter.

- Don't read EVERY tweet.

- Follow anyone who follows you (and unfollow spammers).

- Promote other people 12x to every 1 self-promotional tweet.

- Build lists to watch people who matter to you more closely.

- Retweet the good stuff from others. Sharing is caring.

- A lot of @replies shows a lot of humanity and engagement.

- Robot tweets are less effective than human tweets.

- Promote the new/less followed authors more than the well-established "names."

- Set an egg timer. Twitter is addictive.

- Everyone tweets their own way. You're doing it wrong, too - to someone.

The same principles that apply to social media apply to social networking in general, especially in terms of building up a group of readers who are keen to hear about your publishing plans.

Search out people in the book world as you did online. Target your searches to find the people with the biggest followings in your genre. Once you find them, you can start looking through the list of who they are following to find more people to follow. Build up your followers, which takes time, hence my advice on planning a launch well in advance. Even if you have already launched, set up your profile and spend time regularly building followers.

Search the list pages too. There are many eBook review groups and eBook re-tweeting groups. Some will have over 100,000 followers so if they pick up one of your promotional tweets and pass it on, the results are incredible. There are many writers and publishers who you can follow for great information and tips. Try to find lists created by experts in your field and re-tweet any useful links to your followers.

If we assume that you are now following important people in your niche, you should check them out on a daily basis. Remember to keep adding followers too. Keep your focus tight at first so you don't overwhelm yourself with input. Read the tweets from these industry leaders and add the people with lots of followers. Click through anything that looks interesting to see what they are linking to. Watch especially for links that get re-tweeted or passed along.

There's no rush. I read tweets for two or three months before I sent out any tweets of my own. Be patient and keep watching and soon you'll see why some people are popular and lots of people want to follow them. It is usually because they consistently provide links and ideas that are valuable; or because they make an effort to connect with people individually.

Once you've worked out what's considered valuable in the communities you're following, it's time to become a participant. Do a little searching and see if you can find resources that have not been mentioned recently and pass it on. If you use your Facebook account to post links then it'll automatically send it to Twitter and LinkedIn. Create a short tweet alerting people to this resource, put in a shortened link and tweet it. You will pick up followers if your content is useful.

Re-tweet other authors as this builds brand loyalty. This is all about sharing discoveries, sharing content and not about direct selling. You are building trust and a trusted community of followers; at the same time you are receiving valuable tips from the people you are following.

Be polite to all even when abuse is tweeted in your direction. There are thousands of trolls out there with nothing better to do than annoy people on the internet. If you encounter them, be professional. You will gain the respect of the rest of the community if you handle yourself with dignity. Remember that others can see your conversations unless they are private messages and abusive arguments in clear view of the community will alienate your readers.

In essence, you are asking people that you never met to trust you and read your eBook. This is done most effectively by adding value to others and not by tweeting anything you have not personally verified yourself. Trust is the most important element in the community you are building.

Twitter is truly an amazing phenomenon, considering it only consists of 140 characters of basic text. Become familiar with posting links and photographs. They will create interest in you and your book. The creativity, the energy and vitality on Twitter are astonishing. It can be a great place to connect to people who are interested in your work, and who in turn will send your message out into their own networks of followers.

Join LinkedIn and follow the same rules as the Facebook tips. Remember that LinkedIn is a professional site for executives and senior management from every industry. There are a multitude of author groups, publishers groups, self-publishers, agents and marketing forums. The site gives you the facility to invite everyone in your email address list to join your network by simply clicking one button. The author groups and marketing forums are extremely vibrant and useful.

Join marketing groups and as many book-related forums as you can. Set aside half an hour everyday to participate in the forums. Read the discussions in the marketing forums as there are hundreds of people asking the same questions as you are. There is a plethora of information to be learned on this site and people are very quick to point out any pitfalls that they have fallen into. Learning from other authors' mistakes is a valuable exercise.

Link your LinkedIn account to your Twitter and Facebook accounts. They will syncronise at the click of an icon which saves you a lot of time and effort. These channels thrive on authentic social interactions, so be careful not to overtly sell yourself or your eBook to avoid alienating the connections you make. For example, rather than posting multiple messages about your eBook being available for sale, try to contribute meaningful dialogue in conversations about relevant and related topics. This will position you as an intelligent writer, which will help build your author brand.

Be careful not to hassle agents and publishers. I have seen some cringe-worthy conversations between disparaging, know-it-all writers and not-so desperate agents. They tend to be short, one-sided affairs with abrupt endings!

Talk about your eBook in an open forum intelligently and realistically. Don't claim to have sold 10k. copies of your eBook when your Amazon ranking proves that you have sold ten. You can share any genuine reviews that you receive and post links to your eBook which gives your target audience the chance to glance at your work and make up their own minds as to its merits.

LinkedIn is a useful tool for making business connections and meeting other authors but remember that it is just another tool in the box. Even the most active users miss on some simple ways to optimize the way they use LinkedIn.

Below are a few more tips on how to make the most of your LinkedIn presence.

a) **Think about your goals.** Why are you on LinkedIn. Is it to find new readers and other authors? To be found? Some mix of the two? Your goals should drive your entire presence on the site.

b) **Post a picture of your face.** You should have a professional looking headshot as your LinkedIn photo so people can put a name to a face. If you're uncomfortable with readers or prospective agents seeing your picture next to your professional credentials (a valid concern), you can change your privacy settings so only your connections can see your photo.

c) **Use LinkedIn to help remember names.** LinkedIn can help you with offline networking too. Simply checking on someone's profile after meeting them at a networking event, even if you don't connect, can help you remember their name and what they do. This is another reason why having a picture is important—it will help people remember you.

d) **Make the most of your LinkedIn headline.** Your headline does not have to be your job title alone. Keep it concise, but make sure that it conveys what you do and what your skills are.

e) **Post status.** Updating your status gives you visibility on your connections' LinkedIn home page. If you have found something online you think your business connections would like, or you have good news to share about your work, spread the word by posting it on LinkedIn.

f) **Write a content rich but concise summary.** Your summary should be about you, not your book. Use concrete details like results you have generated and the work you do on a daily basis to *show* people how professional you are, not *tell* them.

g) **Explore various LinkedIn applications.** Add Amazon's Reading List application to your LinkedIn profiles. If you are not sure how the fiction you read is relevant to your professional connections, think again. I get more comments on this list than anything else in my profile.

h) **Add sections to your profile.** LinkedIn offers several sections beyond the standards so users can showcase their volunteer experience, projects, foreign languages, even test scores. This is especially helpful for new networkers who may not have extensive work experience outside of writing a book. Adding more sections can add weight to any profile.

i) Connect with care. Your network is only as valuable as the strength of your connections. For some professionals, it is advantageous to connect generally, but I tend to favour smaller useful lists. If you would like to connect with someone and think it might be a stretch, be sure to personalize the message you send with the invite to explain why you want to connect and why this person should want to connect with you.

j) Join and participate in discussion groups. Some groups are full of spam, drivel and dross, but others are generally valuable. For example, in the book marketing groups there are great places to get and give free advice. Do a little research, think back to your goals, and you'll likely find groups that will help you reach them. If you can't find a group, just start one!

There are many similar general-interest networks like MySpace, Ning, and Bebo, and video sharing websites like YouTube which are essential as you progress, each with different functions and advantages. YouTube is ideal for posting book trailers, linking to any footage of television appearances or advertising clips you produce yourself promoting your eBook.

If you're planning a series of books with a serial protagonist, try creating a Facebook or Twitter account for your protagonist and hold conversations in the voice of that character. The Jack Reacher (Lee Child) forums are constantly busy with readers and avid fans discussing the fictional hero as if he's real. It is not everyone's cup of tea but it works for several authors.

There are networks designed to connect business professionals such as Plaxo, Ryze and most recently BranchOut (a Facebook/LinkedIn hybrid). You can target some networks based on the content of your book. Follow the steps for your Facebook profile. The sites are linked so you might as well take full advantage of the exposure they can offer.

Link with as many other authors as you can. To communicate with other authors and avid readers, try Shelfari or weRead where you can rate, review, and discuss your book, as well as books by other authors. Use Meetup to find and join groups united by a common interest such as politics, books, games, movies, careers, or hobbies. Sites like Digg, Pinterest, Delicious, StumbleUpon, Buzzfeed, Slashdot and Reddit are social bookmarking services for storing, sharing and discovering popular content. Find and use the best ones for your book

Affiliate programs offered by sites like ClickBank and Tradebit can also help you to market your eBook as they provide online marketplaces for digital information products. The sites aim to serve as a connection between digital content creators (known as "vendors") and affiliate marketers, who then promote the relevant content to consumers.

Don't spend much on Google adwords and other "pay-per-click" traffic generators. I have seen campaigns run by authors who have a lot more marketing money than most fall flat on their face. Remember that free advertising is the best way to raise your literary profile and build up a readership for your eBook.

Blogging and vBlogging

You need a good blog because people want "conversation" about the topic of your eBook. It will also help you in Google ratings. A blog builds relationships and credibility. I tend to use Facebook for short daily updates as they are shared automatically with my other sites and then if people are interested in my posts, they will interact. This is a great way for building up links with both readers and writers. You can use your blog to build your platform, exposure, and credibility as an expert on your topic. Keep it authentic, post to it regularly and respond to visitor comments quickly and professionally.

If you cannot commit to writing a regular blog, consider creating occasional content for other blogs which pertain to the topic of your book. Reach out to similar bloggers for guest blog opportunities, and invite them to be a guest on your blog. To get started blogging, consider using a template provided by services like Wordpress, and feature your blog on your website.

Some authors find video blogs (or vBlogs) useful in selling their eBooks. There are three main components. The first is vBlog software. There are a number of options in this regard. Blogger is commonly used by many as it is a free and hosted service, but to make Blogger work you'll have to know or learn some basic computer programming (HTML). Alternatively, if you're willing to pay a nominal fee, you can try TypePad which has more features and is easier to use.

The second component is another hosted service called vBlog Central which hosts photos and videos, automatically converts the videos into Windows, QuickTime, and Real formats, and can automatically link them to your blog.

The third part is actually creating the video itself, preferably with a digital video camcorder with professional editing functionality so that you can ensure your video is the best it can be.

Remember, whatever promotional material you decide to release in support of your eBook will be a reflection on your eBook. If you produce an unedited, unprofessional Youtube video or vBlog to showcase your book, it can put readers off. If you own a shop and have an amateurish-looking shop window display, it's not going to draw people in. Your promotion should be as professional as your book display.

Reviews and Endorsements

Get your eBooks reviewed by as many friends and family members as you can. EBooks with published reviews and real testimonials from various eBook stores or your readers tend to get more attention and interest and thus sell more. I try and reply to every review, good or bad. If it is good then you can build a rapport with the reviewer which tends to generate more positive reviews from them in the future.

If they are scathing then either ignore it or be polite and thank them for the time they spent reading your book. I have seen hilarious discussion threads between wounded authors and reviewers. Some of them are very heated and almost abusive but at the end of the day their opinion is just that, their opinion. You cannot change that.

One best-selling thriller writer was banned from Amazon recently because of his constant battles and criticism of negative reviewers. The long-term result was that the author turned hundreds, if not thousands of potential readers, off his books. As mentioned earlier, your brand is both you and the book. If they don't like you, then they won't buy, endorse or recommend your books, it's simple as that.

Bundling Content & Give-aways

Offer limited period discounts and create bundles. Just like any e-commerce product, an eBook can be offered at a reduced rate for a short time or combine with related products to increase the overall value or worth of the deal to the user.

Build a loyal customer base with a plan to write a series of novels and let people know that there will be more to come. Listen to your readers and give them what they ask for. One main virtue of publishing eBooks is you can turn them out much quicker than traditionally published books. And if you're adept enough to develop an avid fan base, you have the benefit of knowing exactly what they want next.

On a related note, communicate directly with your readers, and communicate with them often. Write back to each of the fans who have written to you over the years — keep all of their messages — to let them know about the book and your plans for your next book. Listen to your avid readers, keep them happy and they'll return to buy your books time and time again.

Another marketing strategy is to give away the first chapter free on sites like Mass-EBooks but include a bold link and a call to action in the chapter telling people how to buy the rest of the eBook. Make sure that you do this for a limited period, as free or discounted offers for eBooks that seem to go on and on can actually diminish your brand name.

Summary

Building up an online community around your profiles takes time and effort but it is worth every minute that you invest. Dedicate time every day to interact with your friends and followers and keep your posts interesting and professional and you will endear readers to try your work.

Introduction

For your book to reach its readers and for you to be a commercially successful author, you need to market yourself as well as your book, which means communicating the message that you want others to hear about your books to a plethora of audiences over a sustained period of time. You have dedicated considerable time and effort to putting your thoughts down in words for others to read, enjoy and learn from, now you need to spread the word, grow your brand and convert readers into fans who will tell their friends and buy your next book.

Building Yourself Up as a Brand Name

Branding is something people hear a lot about but don't fully understand how complex it can be. Examples of good branding are BMW, Microsoft and Virgin. If you buy a product with their brand name on it, you are expecting it to be reliable and great quality. If you shop for beans at Aldi or Lidl, you know the products will be good but perhaps not the same quality as beans from Sainsbury's.

A classic example of poor branding is when Gerald Ratner, Chief Executive of the once profitable Ratners Group of jewellers, made a speech at the Institute of Directors in London in April 1991, and commented:

"We do cut-glass sherry decanters complete with six glasses on a silver-plated tray that your butler can serve you drinks on, all for £4.95. People say, 'How can you sell this for such a low price?' I say, 'Because it's total crap.'"

He compounded this by going on to remark that some of their earrings were "Cheaper than an M&S prawn sandwich but probably wouldn't last as long."

He was joking at the time, but Ratners' shareholders were not laughing for long. Ratner's comments are textbook examples of how you can alienate your target market with substandard quality and off-the-cuff remarks. Consumers exacted their revenge by staying away from Ratner shops. The value of Ratners Group plummeted by £500 million, which nearly lead to the company's collapse. Ratner subsequently resigned in November 1992 and the group changed its name to Signet Group in September 1993 because the "Ratner" brand had suffered immeasurably from this marketing faux-pas.

It takes a lot of time and promotional work to establish yourself as an author and a brand name by following the tips set out in this guide, but only a few minutes to lose that hard-won credibility and fan base either by publishing books that have not been professionally proofread or making caustic remarks on discussion boards or on Amazon as one well-known crime writer did recently in criticising reviewers of his book, which lead Amazon to throw his own books off the site for a period of time, costing him both readers and revenue.

As an author, you cannot separate yourself from your books completely even if you use a pen-name, because you still have to work with people who will be aware of the author's real name. In fact, writing under a pen-name can limit your marketing activities in some ways. Likewise, uploading positive reviews of your book disguised as "anonymous" postings on discussion boards or adding five-star reviews of your book on Amazon can detract rather than enhance your book's marketing reach because it's obvious which glowing, detailed reviews are written by authors, especially those that say "a must-read" and "I cannot wait for the author's next book."

Having said that, it seems as if the majority of first reviews for books on Amazon are 5* and written by the author, or a close relative or friend, per the author's request. In some respects, it's better for the first review to be 3* or 4* as it tends to lend more credibility to the review. I remember an author acquainted with Piers Morgan telling me that he asked Piers to write an endorsement for the back cover of his book, to which Piers replied, "I'd be glad to provide a positive review, just don't expect me to read it!" Orchestrating positive reviews is of little use to you or your book as honest, genuine feedback, whether good, bad or average, will give you a much better understanding of the strengths and shortcomings of your book. By all means encourage reviews from readers as part of your book promotion to build up a brand name and fan base, but don't fabricate them.

Similarly, a number of authors including the aforementioned writer who was thrown off Amazon for a spell for criticizing and to some extent threatening negative reviewers, admitted that he has been actively posting adverse reviews of other crime writers' books on Amazon and the like, thereby causing their books to move down the "recommended reading" lists on Amazon, a baneful practice known as "sockpuppeting". Once exposed in a national newspaper for doing this, surprisingly along with a number of other well-known authors in various genres, he decided to "go to ground" and likely lost some of his readers as well as his credibility. Not only was he undermining other authors in this self-centred way, but he shot himself squarely in the foot in doing so, damaging his author brand.

If you disrespect your readers or other writers, criticise your publisher for not doing more, upload raving reviews of your own book or harass retailers for not stocking your book, then no one will want to work with you and your books won't have a chance. Conversely, if your readers take time out of their busy schedules to review your book, even negatively, you should consider carefully what they say and respond positively to them. Do not take your readers for granted, or you will lose them quicker than you gained them. Listen closely to your readers, and give them what they're asking for.

Having warned of the potential pitfalls that you should avoid, let's turn to what you *should* be doing to build an author brand. You and your books make up your brand. Your books are your logo and will be your readers' first impression of you, hence it is vital that you get the title and the covers right. Along with the story-lines that you skilfully and painstakingly weave together, your author brand is how you pitch your work and how you conduct yourself.

Good examples of branding in the literary world are Mills and Boon. Everyone knows that they publish romantic novels. Stephen King is a horror and thriller writer that most people will know which is why his name is much larger than the title on his last five books. Julia Donaldson is author of over 120 children's books and on the cover of many of them it states in bold "by the Children's Laureate and author of *The Gruffalo*". I took my children to see Julia Donaldson speak at the Wonderlands Festival of Writing at the British Library and expected a question-and-answer session with the author talking about herself, her inspiration behind writing best-loved children's stories, and what she's working on next. Instead, she skilfully engaged and involved most all of the hundred+ children in the audience over the course of an hour and invited them to act out her stories while she sang songs from her books, accompanied by her multi-talented guitar-playing husband, Malcolm.

J. K. Rowling has set a great example to writers by playing down her success and being pragmatic during interviews. Many people will know that she wrote her early novels in cafes in Edinburgh because the walk there helped get her young daughter to sleep and that she was a single mother at the time. Her brand is her Harry Potter novels first, and her personal "rags to riches" life story has added to her overall brand because she came from humble beginnings and downplays her success. You are your brand. Get people to like you and they will want to read your books.

Forget about your book as the focus for a moment and concentrate on building up yourself as a brand. You've probably heard of the term "personal branding." It's a phrase popular with personal development types that means "how you present yourself to the world." This obviously applies to the literary and business world and also to your extended circle of contacts. The main idea is that whether you like it or not, the world is going to have an opinion about you which will be manufactured from how you conduct yourself in the public arena. Most people don't think too much about how they're seen by others but if you put yourself out there, then you will be judged. That is just human nature. You can no longer just live and let the world think of you however they'd like.

"Personal branding" is about intentionally influencing how the world sees you by behaving in a certain manner. It's about purposefully packaging that "brand called you," making sure it is a likable package, so much so that your readers want to "buy into it". The benefits are obvious. The better prepared you are to show the world who you are, the more likely the world will see you the way you want them to. Being respectful and positive adds value to your book and increases your fan base, thereby adding value to your author brand.

That means your readers and reviewers.

That means interviewers from the media.

That means people searching for you and your books online.

That means your social circle, family, friends and other professionals from the literary world.

When you have a solid personal brand, you'll be more memorable, you'll be more impressive, and people will end up having a more favourable opinion about you. They will be much more likely to go away and look at your book and subsequently upload a favourable review if they like you – that's the same thing that good branding does for a product.

How to Actually Do It In Practice

Like most things in the world of personal development, "personal branding" is a pretty vague concept. It is a great idea in theory but how do you sit down and plan how to do it?

It's one of those things that sound nice, but discussions about it tend to be impractical or not actionable enough to be useful. If an idea isn't practical, is it worth much? Here are some basic tips to help you develop a brand name. Follow these six easy steps or adapt them to suit your own situation and you'll have worked out a personal brand strategy that you can start building on straight away:

Step 1: Choose the core focus for your personal brand

Every brand is based on a few memorable qualities which marketing people tend to focus on. For instance, BMW don't market their vehicles on their green credentials or their safety record. They market them on their quality and contemporary styling and up to the minute technology. Focusing on a few key qualities makes it easier to connect and remember the product it's attached to.

Another good example of branding is Apple. Apple sells computers, phones, and software. You could say a lot about them, but their brand is focused. Apple's brand is fun, slick, stylish, cutting-edge, reliable, and virus-free. Their brand is focused and it's positive. You need to do the same. Choose a handful of qualities about yourself that you want to be known for. Maybe you're a children's book author and when you write blogs or interact with people you come over as someone who cares about children, or maybe you are an excellent reviewer of other children's books. Or maybe you're a confident speaker, detail oriented, serious about important issues and a crazy JK Rowling fan.

What core attributes do you want to be known for by the world? Obviously you want to be known for your books. Make sure you don't try to focus on too many things – it'll be harder for someone to remember any of it. Concentrate on two key aspects and maybe three or four minor ones. Make sure you're honest with yourself – pretending to be something you're not never works and there are many trolls out there who will see through you and take great pleasure in dissecting your mistakes in the public eye.

So, firstly, write down the 4 or 5 things you want the world to know about you.

Step 2: Prioritize your core brand focus

It's easier for people to remember one thing than several things. It's easier for people to focus on doing one thing than doing a lot of things. For example, most websites want their visitors to do a variety of things – get on an email list, bookmark the site, click on an advert, buy a product, comment, share on social media, etc. The more of those things a website focuses on, the less likely visitors are to do anything but go to a different website. Too many options lead to inaction. The same concept is true for your personal branding. The more you throw at someone, the less likely they are to remember any of it. So what you have to do is look at your list of 4 or 5 qualities about yourself and decide which of them is the most important. If someone could define you by one quality, which would it be?

The other apects of your character, though important, can be secondary elements in your personal brand.

Rank your 4 or 5 elements by importance to you.

Step 3: Make your core values into priority list

As a general rule, people talk up the importance of things like personal goals and objectives, and personal mission statements too much. Even so, the process of developing a key list helps take something general (like a list of 5 qualities about you) and makes it easier to talk about convincingly. That's important, because it can be hard to talk about something you haven't already thought through. When some asks you what you do, you need to be able to sum up your core values in a few interesting sentences.

Have you ever talked about something in public without first having time to think about what you had to say? For example, has someone ever asked you to tell a story about something funny that happened to you? You remembered exactly what happened, but it comes out in a jumble. So you try to explain your funny story, but your friends' eyes glaze over because you're not telling it well, and you eventually end awkwardly with, "Oh, well, I guess you had to have been there for it to be funny."

It's a similar situation with your personal brand. You need to think through how to communicate it or it won't be useful.

Here's the best way to work through that quickly:

1) Pull up something that can record audio on your computer or phone.
2) Literally record yourself talking about each of your 4 to 5 qualities, why they are important, why other people should think they're important, and examples that would show the world you have them.
3) Ramble on and on until your ideas start solidifying. Talk until it starts feeling more comfortable and natural to talk about them.
4) Once you start feeling comfortable with what you're saying, stop recording, and listen to it.
5) Write down the most compelling things you said – the things you think are the smartest, most eloquent things you said about yourself.
6) Condense the best stuff into three sentences that emphasize your primary quality while including the others. This is your "elevator pitch" for the purpose of this exercise.
7) Actually work through your words, making mental notes, and distilling it into your core values. Don't stress about getting this perfect. This an exercise in narrowing down the excess so you have a convincing paragraph of information which will be your core focus. If you practice it, it will become more convincing.

Step 4: Focus your online identity with your new core statement

Like it or not, what you do online influences how others perceive you and also your product. If you want your personal brand to be effective, your online accounts at Facebook, Twitter, LinkedIn and your other online profiles need to reflect the ideas in your core statement from Step 3. If you were a stranger looking at your online accounts, would your main message reflect your personal brand? If you look at Conrad Jones' Facebook account or fan page, you know straight away that he is a thriller writer. He doesn't post what he is having for breakfast or what new trick his dog learned today, but he does post every review that he carries out or receives. If you visit it then you would be under no illusions that he is an author.

If your Facebook account or blog doesn't do this, then you need to think about adjusting things that you have online and take your time to get it right and stick to those key focal points. Don't cut and paste your core statement into your Facebook profile as that would look unprofessional and somewhat retentive. Instead, emphasize the things that make your personal author brand stronger online and de-emphasize the things that conflict with it. For example, if you say you're a published author and reviewer, delete any quotes you might have on the site about disliking someone's book or criticizing traditional publishers and agents for not having the courtesy to reply to your book submissions or sending templated rejection letters rather than providing constructive feedback.

Take a quick audit of your online profiles and start adjusting things so they reflect the elements of your personal brand and concentrate on the core ideals.

Step 5: Take more control of your online brand identity

Most companies have a presence on social media nowadays that reflect their brand. But their online platform is a website they own. The reason for that is simple. You can manage your online profiles, but you have complete control over a website you own. The same is true for you. You can clean up your Facebook account all you want, but if you really want to solidify your brand online, creating a personal website is the best way to make that happen, as it provided a professional platform to showcase for your writing, sort of like a shop window for your online bookshop.

This step might take you off-guard a little. Many people think creating their own website is difficult, or they might need to learn complex computer programming, or they'd need to pay thousands of pounds to get someone to design a website for them. The truth is that it's never been easier or less expensive to create your own website these days. If you're knowledgeable enough to have bought this book online then you are already computer literate enough to create your own website. If you don't know and want more details about how to easily create your own author website, go to www.WebsiteFromNothing.com.

It has a quick, useful series of tutorial videos that show you how to do it.

We recommend you build your website on a domain based on your name (rather than your book title) for the most effective personal branding. If your name was John Crowther, buy www.johncrowther.com, .net, or .org. The .com suffix is generally the most important one to have, as it gives your writing more international kudos. Often, authors' names with a .com suffix have already been taken by someone else, so you may need to be slightly more creative by adding in your middle initial so it would be www.johnccrowther.com or if you'd prefer, add –author to your website domain name, so that it might be www.johncrowther-author.com. That tells people right on the tin that you are an author.

Then make sure your site is simple and clearly highlights your personal brand. It should clearly show your core focus. It should communicate, "This is who I am, this is what I write, and this is why you should read it." Be creative and take your time to update and improve your pages. It's your online real estate.

Create your own personal website to establish your personal branding.

Step 6: Live your personal core brand

The last and most important step is to live your personal brand. A personal brand should be more than how you present yourself to the world. It should also be a real life description of why you're who you say you are. So that's what you should be. Spend your time emphasizing the core elements of your personal brand in your life. Sometimes we don't act like the person we want the world to see. We think we're motivated, but we spend too much time watching television and surfing the internet. If you post yourself as an author and reviewer, then write every day, post interesting reviews and people will see that you are an active author and reviewer, rather than passively waiting for people to find you.

A well thought out personal brand will help you present yourself to the world. It can also be a clear cut description of who you should aspire to be in your day-to-day life. No matter whom you are or what your goals may be, it is helpful to go through these simple steps and develop your personal identity and brand and concentrate on the core ideals on a daily basis. Decide that it's going to be an integral part of your marketing strategy. If you get it right then you can use it to your advantage in raising your literary profile and building up a readership for your writing. Are you going to sit and hope that readers come to you by chance or are you are going to go out and grab their interest?

Summary

To recap the Do's and Don'ts in successfully building an author brand name:

Do's:

a) Have your book professionally proofread prior to publication.
b) Encourage reviews from your readers and especially your fan base.
c) Thank reviewers for taking the time to review your book, whether the review is positive or otherwise.

Don't:

a) Resist uploading or orchestrating 5* reviews of your own book to Amazon.
b) Avoid uploading negative reviews of other authors' books or engaging in sockpuppeting.
c) Never make caustic remarks on discussion boards or on Amazon.
d) Be careful not to disrespect your readers or other aspiring writers.

Make sure that all your profile pages reflect what you want to say about yourself. Audit your pages to minimise the clutter and focus on your core values. Remember to stay focused and professional at all times even when dealing with scathing remarks or poor reviews. What you write will not be liked by everyone, focus on the positives and take any criticism as an opportunity to improve. If you take it personally, it will grind you down. Keep positive, interact daily and keep writing. Brand building does not happen overnight. It takes a lot of time, effort and commitment, just like your writing.

Conrad Jones

Conrad started writing as a business venture. It was a change of career, not an artistic project. Although he eventually achieved a respectable income from his books, things were not simple in the beginning and he learned some harsh lessons along the way. Based on his varied experiences in selling and promoting his own eBooks, Conrad explains to authors the things that worked and the things that didn't. He had no agent to start and no publisher to guide and support his efforts. Rather, he learned the hard way, through trial and error.

It was a back-to-front journey but the success of his eBook sales earned him the interest of a good agent and a publishing deal. If you can follow the simple guidelines and tips set out in this book then you can build sales and prove to the traditional industry that you are a saleable asset in the literary world. Or, if you prefer, you can choose to go it alone and still make a decent residual monthly income.

When Conrad turned his paperbacks into eBooks, his thriller series stormed the kindle charts. Within 3 weeks of launching them, he had two titles (*The Child Taker* and *Slow Burn*) in the top ten kindle lists. Not genre lists, the overall sales chart. All seven of his thrillers were in the top 40 for nearly 12 months. On the release of his 8th book (*Nine Angels*), it flew to number 3 in the horror charts overnight. *The Child Taker* was number 1 in thriller law books and *Tank* was number 1 in thriller war books. He achieved over 120,000 digital downloads in the first year. It wasn't just luck. Rather, it was the success of building a marketing base over a period of years and then applying everything that he had learned to the launch of his eBooks. His credentials are actual book sales, a growing fan base and over 250 five-star reviews across the *Soft Target* series.

Bibliography of Author guides to marketing and publishing

100 ways to publish and sell your own eBook and make it a bestseller
(the number 1 bestselling book marketing guide in 3 different genres on kindle)

UK VERSIONS

http://www.amazon.co.uk/Ways-Publish-Sell-E-Book-ebook/dp/B00A6DCZWW/ref=sr_1_1?s=digital-text&ie=UTF8&qid=1361961741&sr=1-1

How to market an eBook

http://www.amazon.co.uk/How-Market-Your--book-ebook/dp/B00B0XMA5E/ref=sr_1_2?s=digital-text&ie=UTF8&qid=1361961838&sr=1-2

How to publish an eBook

http://www.amazon.co.uk/How-Market-Your--book-ebook/dp/B00B0XMA5E/ref=sr_1_2?s=digital-text&ie=UTF8&qid=1361961838&sr=1-2

USA VERSIONS

http://www.amazon.com/Ways-Publish-Sell-E-Book-

BOOK TITLE

ebook/dp/B00A6DCZWW/ref=sr_1_1?s=digital-text&ie=UTF8&qid=1361962003&sr=1-1&keywords=100+ways+to+publish

http://www.amazon.com/How-Market-Your-book-ebook/dp/B00B0XMA5E/ref=sr_1_3?s=digital-text&ie=UTF8&qid=1361962042&sr=1-3

http://www.amazon.com/How-To-Publish--book-ebook/dp/B00B121NEI/ref=sr_1_1?s=digital-text&ie=UTF8&qid=1361962042&sr=1-1

WEBSITES AND SOCIAL MEDIA LINKS

Amazon author page

http://www.amazon.co.uk/Conrad-Jones/e/B002BOBGRE/ref=ntt_dp_epwbk_0

Facebook fan page

http://www.facebook.com/conradjonesauthorpage

Twitter

https://twitter.com/ConradJones

CPSIA information can be obtained at www.ICGtesting.com
Printed in the USA
LVOW06s1711020614

388251LV00007B/1457/P

9 781482 656787